SEVERAL ASSERTIONS PROVED, IN ORDER TO CREATE ANOTHER SPECIES OF MONEY THAN GOLD AND SILVER

J. ASGILL

RE–ISSUED IN A SERIES OF REPRINTS OF
CLASSIC ENGLISH WORKS ON
THE HISTORY AND DEVELOPMENT OF
ECONOMIC THOUGHT
UNDER THE EDITORIAL DIRECTION OF
PROFESSOR W. E. MINCHINTON
UNIVERSITY OF EXETER

S. R. PUBLISHERS LIMITED
JOHNSON REPRINT CORPORATION

1970

This reproduction has been made with the kind permission of the Goldsmiths' Librarian, University of London, from the copy held in the Goldsmiths' Library, Senate House, London, W.C. 1.

The publishers would like to acknowledge the assistance of Dr. J. H. P. Pafford, M.A., F.S.A., F.L.A., the former Goldsmiths' Librarian, Miss M. B. C. Canney of the Goldsmiths' Library and Mr. F. J. Bosley, M.I.R.T., the chief photographer to the Goldsmiths' Library, without whose assistance this series of reprints could not have been successfully under taken.

Library of Congress Catalog Card Number: 70-133312

British Standard Book Number: 85409-235-8

S. R. Publishers Ltd.
East Ardsley, Wakefield
Yorkshire, England

Johnson Reprint Corporation
111 Fifth Avenue
New York, N.Y. 10003, U.S.A.

Printed in the U.S.A.

SEVERAL ASSERTIONS PROVED,

In Order to Create another

Species of MONEY

THAN

GOLD

AND

SILVER.

SEVERAL ASSERTIONS PROVED, &c.

First Assertion.

That there seemeth a Necessity of creating another Species of Money than Gold and Silver.

BY Necessity I don't mean an absolute Necessity, but such a Necessity that either this must be done, or a worse thing will ensue for want of it. The past Contracts *Proved.*

now depending in the Kingdom for payment of Moneys in Specie do far surmount all the Species of Money in the Kingdom; and because Money is become more valuable than Bills of Credit, therefore they that have the demands of it do and will demand it; and the more they demand it, the higher the price rises, so that the price multiplies the demands, and the demands advance the price, which renders the performance of these past Contracts to be impossible: And thus the Kingdom stands Stock-jobbed, by being obliged to deliver what they have not: And yet these Contracts (tho' they are impossible to be performed) are lawful, for by the Law where the Condition of a Bond is impossible, the Bond it self is absolute, and the Obligee may sue for the Penalty, and have Judgment; and

and if (in this Case) the Plaintiffs happen to be more than the Defendants, they may have Execution too; but if the Defendants come to be more than the Plaintiffs, there's an end of the Law.

And notwithstanding that the whole Moneys of the Kingdom stand anticipated by the past Contracts, the present Exigencies and the growing Contracts call for as much more, and 'tis impossible to answer these Demands but by the Money due on the former Contracts, taking it from whence 'tis already due, and lending it to the present Wants; and thus the Publick have had the greatest part of their late Supplyes, (which I don't observe as a misapplication of the Moneys, (under our Necessities) but as an Evidence of our Necessities) *Therefore for preserving the peace of the Kingdom, in relation to the past Contracts, and for raising the present and future Supplyes, there doth seem a Necessity of creating another Species of Money than Gold and Silver.*

Second Assertion.

That this Necessity is no Cause to discourage Proceedings in publick or private Affairs, but rather to force us upon an Invention which otherwise we should not find out.

Proved. All the Improvements in the World have been produced from the Necessities of Men, putting them upon Invention, according to that saying, *Venter largitor Artium*: Shame invented our Cloathing, Cold our Houses, Hunger our Food,

Food, Sickneſs our Phyſick, and Rapine our Laws; Laws neceſſitated Trade, Trade neceſſitated Money, and the multiplyed occaſions for Money doth now put us upon a neceſſity of inventing another Species of it, and therefore we muſt find it out. What if the *Spaniards* Mines were exhauſted, or the Laws of their Countrey (prohibiting the Exportation of them) obſerved, muſt the whole World ſtand ſtill? As Silver and Gold were invented for Money, when they were to be had, ſo when we cann't have that, we muſt invent ſomething elſe (which may be had) inſtead of it. The whole World once lay open for Man and Beaſts to be Tenants in common of it all, but while it lay ſo, it was incapable of improvement, becauſe no Man could preſerve the benefit of his own Labour to himſelf, and this forced men upon Agreements to incloſe, and that every Man ſhould have a Property in his own Incloſure, which was the firſt initiating of Laws, and this Law forced Trade. For the Earth conſiſting of divers Veins, of different qualities, diſtant from one another, one man came to have occaſion of ſomething which lay in (*alieno ſolo*) another man's Incloſure, and ſo they exchanged with one another; but the things exchanged not being always equal in value, nor to be delivered at the ſame time and place, put men upon an Invention of Pledges, or ſecurity for the things delivered, until the value thereof ſhould be returned in another Commodity; and theſe at firſt were but particular Tokens between one man and another, 'till by degrees Silver and Gold (having acquired a certain

certain value from the uſes made of it for other things) became the common pledge of the World, and by further degrees the Values thereof came to be aſcertained by Laws, which hath advanced it to an extravagant price, contrary to the original intention of it. The ſole uſe of Money (as Money) is but to keep an Account of other things by; it is a Tool in Trade found out by the Policy of Man, and that it might not grow into any other uſe, the firſt Law of the World (foreſeeing the miſchief) forbid thoſe that had it, from taking Intereſt for the Loan of it, from any but thoſe whom they deſigned to impoveriſh by it: But ſince this prohibited uſe of it hath advanced it above its original inſtitution, we muſt invent ſomething elſe inſtead of it, as they who had the firſt Occaſions of Money did invent Gold and Silver: *And therefore this Necessity is no Cause to discourage us from proceeding in publick or private Affairs, but rather to force us upon an Invention which otherwise we should not find out.*

Third Assertion.

That all Proposals for making Bills of Credit current Money directly, by Act of Parliament, can be of no use in this Invention.

Proved. For, 1. *These Proposals are Unjust*, being more than the Law doth in relation to the Coyns of the Kingdom. The Law never makes the Coyns of the Kingdom to be current in any Payments but where they are agreed to be paid, but these Proposals would make these Bills

Bills current in Payments, in which they were never agreed for, therefore they are unjuſt.

2. *They are Illegal*: I mean, they are an Inverſion of Laws, which the Legiſlative Power have no power to do; their Name defines their power not to be abſolute, but only a power of making Laws; and the intent of all Laws being for the preſervation of Life and Property, whatever violates this Intent, is no Law. Should an Act paſs, that every Man in the Kingdom ſhould kill himſelf, or give his Eſtate to any one elſe that would do it for him, this would be no Law, nor any Man's Life or Eſtate bound by it. Now ſome Men have turned their Properties into Land, and ſome into Money, and all by Agreements with one another; and ſhould an Act paſs, that a Man who hath agreed for, and purchaſed 500 *l.*

per

per Annum in Land, ſhould convey that Eſtate to any Man who would pay him 10000 *l.* in Gold or Silver, this would be no Law; then by the ſame parity of Reaſon, ſhould an Act paſs that any Man who hath contracted for 10000 *l.* to be paid him in Money, ſhould aſſign this Contract to any one, who would convey to him 500 *l. per Annum* in Land, this would be no Law; for if ſuch Acts ſhould be admitted as Laws, they put an end to all Laws. Men cann't deal but by Agreements with one another, and if the Law will invert thoſe Agreements, this puts an end to all dealing, *and therefore theſe Propoſals are Illegal*, by which I hope I ſhall not be cenſured as irreverent of the Legiſlative Power, for I mention this in reverence to thoſe Laws of which they are the Legiſlators. I don't ſay, but one Man

may

may by Conqueſt get an abſolute Power over another, but this is by Uſurpation and Wrong, and not by Law; for all Laws are the Agreements of Men, and no Man ever by his own Agreement delivered himſelf into the diſpoſal of an abſolute Power. God himſelf (tho' a ſupream Power, and abſolute over all) doth not demand Man to deliver himſelf up into his Power as abſolute, but treats with him by a Law of Juſtice, in which he makes himſelf a Party, and ſtands obliged to the performance of ſeveral things, as the Condition of Man's Obedience, and therefore for man to aſſume a right of Government by an abſolute Power, is to ſet himſelf above God.

3. *Theſe Propoſals are impracticable*, and (ſhould they be granted) would be ineffectual. Suppoſe an Act ſhould paſs, that a tender

der

der of a Bill of 100 *l.* ſhould be a ſufficient tender of 100 *l.* contracted for in lawful Money of *England*, and the People ſhould think themſelves bound by this as a Law, then their ſtudy would be to evade this Law, by changing their Contracts from lawful Money of *England* to ſome other Species, *As ſo many Ounces of Gold and Silver*, which would not be conſtrued to be lawful Money of *England*, and ſo then the Act would not reach it; and if the Act ſhould follow theſe Contracts, and be changed as often as the Contracts, it muſt at laſt be ſo general, that a tender of a Bill for payment of 10 *l.* ſhould be a good tender for all Commodities agreed to be delivered of the value of 10 *l.* and ſo when a Man had contracted for a Horſe, he ſhould have a Bank Bill delivered him to ride on, *and therefore the Propoſals*

are

are impracticable, and (if granted) would be ineffectual.

4. *These Proposals are fallacious, and carry a Cheat in the bottom*; for the Bills being given out for payment of Money, if the Law releases the payment of the Money, and makes the Bill it self a good tender, there's nothing left to answer the Debt but the Paper or Parchment on which the Bill is written, which is worth nothing, and therefore the Proposals are fallacious, and carry a Cheat in the bottom : *And for all these Reasons they can be of no Use in this Invention, of finding out another Species of Money than Gold and Silver.*

Fourth Aſſertion.

That this Species muſt be made of ſomething that hath all the Qualities of Money.

Proved. Money hath theſe ſeveral Qualities: Firſt, *The Mettal of which it is made is Valuable*, from the other Uſes made of it; for Silver and Gold do not receive their Value from being made Money, but Money receives its value from being made of Silver and Gold: For Money (as Money) hath no other value than Figures or Counters, by which Men keep Accounts with one another; but becauſe Money is now become a common Pledge, it muſt be made of ſomething that hath in it ſelf a real

Value

Value from other Uſes, whereby whoever hath theſe Tokens, may purchaſe any Commodity with them, according to their Value in weight in all other places as well as where the Money was coined, and therefore nothing can be made Money but what is thus valuable, from the other Uſes made of it. *The* Second *Quality of Money is Durableneſs and Incorruption*, which is alſo Neceſſary. *The* Third *Quality is Diviſibleneſs into greater or leſſer peices*, without which it cannot be uſed as Money. Fourthly, *The Value* of each piece is certified by the ſtamp, without which it could not be uſed as Money, by the common People. Fifthly, *The Title thereof is readily transferrable ; the Delivery only makes it a Title* : And this is as neceſſary for making it money as any of the other qualities : For were the Titles of Land tranſ ferred to the Titles of Money, it would ceaſe to be Money, notwithſtanding all its other qualities; were it neceſſary to have a Leaſe and Releaſe, Feofment or Bargain and Sale, and (if it came by the Wife) a Fine, to the Transferre of every peice of money, the Charge and Trouble of this would ſoon reduce our Nobles to Nine-pences. Now all theſe qualities being Neceſſary to Money, nothing that wants either of theſe qualities can be Money, *Therefore this Species muſt be made of ſomething that hath all theſe Qualities.*

Fifth Aſſertion.

That whatever is capable of all theſe Qualities of Money, is capable of being made Money.

The Philoſophers define all Subſtances by Qualites; they ſay, That whatever hath all the qualities of a thing, ceaſes to be a likeneſs, and is become that very thing. Now I don't ſay, that whatever hath all the qualities of Money, doth thereby become Gold and Silver, but it becomes Money. Gold is money, and Silver is money, and yet Gold is not Silver, nor Silver Gold. Things of different Subſtances may be put to the ſame uſe; Brick and Stone, Braſs and Copper, Lead and Iron, may *Proved.*

be all adapted to the ſame Uſes, being ſtamped into the ſame Forms; *Therefore whatever is capable of all the Qualities of Money, is capable of being made Money.*

Sixth Aſſertion.

That the Securities on Lands are capable of all the Qualities of Money, and therefore they are capable of being made Money.

Proved. *Firſt*, The Lands on which the Securities are charged, have in themſelves *a real Value, from the other Uſes made of them*, which need not be enumerated.

Secondly, *They are durable and incorruptible*: The Earth is the great Store-houſe of the World, where all

all the magazines of Life and Defence are kept ſweet and ſafe.

Thirdly, *Theſe Securities are diviſible into greater or leſſer Summs.*

Fourthly, *The Value of each Security may be certified by a ſtamp given to it.*

Fifthly, *The Title of theſe Securities may be transferrable, by delivery only* : And all this is proved by Fact; *And therefore theſe being all the Qualities of Money, and the Securities of Lands being capable of all theſe Qualities, they are capable of being made Money.*

Seventh Aſſertion.

That theſe Securities of Lands being thus formed into the Qualities of Money, it is in the Power of the Owners of the Lands themſelves to make theſe Securities to be Effective *and* Lawful *Money of* England, By reſerving the Rents of their Lands payable in them.

Proved. Firſt, *This would make them effective Money*: The uſe of Money is to buy Commodities, now theſe Securities will buy Land, and therefore they will buy all Commodities. The common definition of Money,

Money, *That 'tis Money that buys Land*, is comprehenſive of all the uſes of it; for whatever will buy Land will buy all Commodities. What we call Commodities is nothing but *Land ſevered from the Soil*: The Owners of the Soil in every Country have the ſale of all Commodities of the Growth of that Country, and conſequently have the power of giving Credit in that Country, and therefore whatever they will accept for their Commodities is Money. Man deals in nothing but Earth; the Merchants are the Factors of the World, to exchange one part of the Earth for another: The King himſelf is fed by the labour of the Ox, and the cloathing of the Army, and the victualing of the Navy, muſt all be paid for to the Owner of the Soil, as the ultimate Receiver, and whatever the ultimate Receiver will demand or accept, must be a Rule for the intermediate Receivers to govern themselves by: All the other Contracts of the Kingdom must follow the Reservation of the Rents; and hence 'tis that all the present Contracts of the Kingdom are agreed to be paid in Money, because the Rents of the Lands are reserved payable in it; and therefore if these Rents were reserved in the Securities of Land, form'd into the Qualities of Monies, (which we call Bills) it would force other Contracts to be made payable in these Bills, *and consequently make these Bills effective Money.*

Secondly, *As they would thereby become effective Money,* so they would become *Lawful Money of England*; because the Law would compel the payment of them. The Law

of

of *England* hath given no other ſanction to Gold or Silver, than to certifie the value of it, to tell the People what it is, that when they make Contracts about it, they may know what they do. The Law ſaith that ſuch a piece of Money, ſtamped into the King's Coin, ſhall be eſteemed five ſhillings of lawful Money of *England*, whereby whoever makes a Contract to pay five ſhillings of lawful Money of *England*, knows what he is to deliver, and he knows that the delivery of that piece will be a good diſcharge of his Contract. But the Law never compels any perſon to make theſe Contracts, nor ever compels the payment of this Money, or makes the tender thereof to be a good payment, in any caſe, but where it ſo agreed between the Parties; and this is no more but what the Law doth to any other thing contracted for, as well as Money: The Law no more admits Gold or Silver Money to be a tender for Corn, or Cattle, contracted to be delivered, then it doth admit Corn or Cattle to be a tender for Gold or Silver Money contracted to be delivered, for the Law respects nothing but the agreement of the Parties; and by the same reason that the Law obliges the payment of Gold and Silver, it would oblige the payment of these Bills, in case they were agreed to be paid: *And therefore it being in the power of the Owners of the Lands, to reserve their Rents payable in these Bills; and the other Contracts of the Kingdom being govern'd by the Reservation of the Rents, and the Law compelling the performance of those Reservations and Contracts, it is in the power of the Owners of the Lands to make these Bills effective and lawful*

ful Money of England, *by reserving their Rents payable in them.*

Eighth Assertion.

That Lands thus formed into the Qualities of Money, are more Useful and Valuable than Gold and Silver, or any other Commodities severed from the Soyl.

First, *They are more Useful*: Gold and Silver serve but for one use at one time, while they are used for Money, they can be used for nothing else, and while they are used for any thing else, they can't be used for Money: But Lands may be converted into Money, without loosing their other Faculties; they serve for both uses at the same time **Proved.**

time, the Owners keep the Possession, and receive the Profits of the Soil, while the Securities thereof are used for Money; and this is what cannot be done in Securities of Pledges, or Pawns of Commodities severed from the Soil; for when the Owner makes these a Security, he must part with them out of his possession, and can make no use of them 'till he hath redeemed them.

2. *As they are more Useful, so they are more Valuable*: What serves for two uses at once, is more valuable than what serves but for one; if Silver and Gold could serve for Money and Plate both at the same time, or if Commodities severed from the Soil, could retain their own natural uses, and also serve for Securities of Money at the same time, they would both be double the value they now are;

for

for by loosing one of their uses, they loose the value at which they are valu'd in respect of that use; therefore Lands retaining their own natural use, while they are made Money, *are more Useful and Valuable than Gold and Silver, or any other Commodity severed from the Soil.*

Ninth Assertion.

That it will be in the Power of the Bank from whom these Bills are issued, to make them more Valuable than other Money, by accepting them at a higher Rate, and that they will be Gainers thereby.

The Profit of a Bank depends upon the Credit of their Bills, and the *Proved.*

the Credit of their Bills depends upon their making them more Valuable than Money; and the making their Bills more valuable than Money depends on their accepting of them at a higher Rate than Money. Money and Bills never keep long at a par; if Bills are not better than Money, they'll ſoon be worſe: If Money gets the upper Hand of Credit, it puts an end to all Credit. There is at this day no Credit in the Kingdom. Credit is when Men chooſe Bills rather than Money, and not when they take them only becauſe they can't receive Money. The preſent Credit of the Kingdom is no more than the Credit of a man who can't pay his Debts, and therefore gives Bond, which his Creditors are forced to accept for want of money. The *Bank* of *England* have iſſued out Bills which they

can-

cannot pay, and ſo the People that have their Bills muſt keep them. But there is no freſh Money brought into their Bank for their Bills, without which no Credit can be maintain'd : And they finding great Demands upon them, immediately raiſed the Intereſt upon their Bills, hoping thereby to keep thoſe Bills which were out againſt them from being demanded of them, and to draw in freſh Monies into them: But this proved ſo ineffectual, that their Bills at Intereſt are at no more value than their Bills without Intereſt, which ſhews plainly, that the giving Intereſt on Bills doth add no Credit to a Bank. For raiſing the intereſt on the Bills of the Bank, raiſes the Intereſt of Monies out of the Bank, and ſo keeps the Monies from them. The more a Bank raiſes their Intereſt

to

to overtake the Money, the faster the Money goes from them, raising the Interest 1 *l. per Cent.* upon Bills payable at demand, raises it 2 *l. per Cent.* on Common Securities; therefore a Bank should always fall their Interest as fast as others endeavour to raise it. Credit is no more to be begged or bought than it is to be forced; giving Interest on Bills is begging of Credit, or buying of Money, which may be done by a common way of mortgaging, (without keeping Monies to pay the principal at demand): And it had been Policy for the Bank of *England* (when they had got the Coin raised from clipt to full Money) to have raised the value of their Bills with it, by accepting them in Reciepts of Interest, from the Crown and others, at more than Money, and then they had kept down

down the Price of Money below their Bills, which is now got above them: For let Money be of what Weight it will, if those who have the Receipt of it, will accept Bills at a higher rate, this doth depreciate the Money, and keeps the Bills above them: And therefore in case this Land-Bank be established by Parliament, (as is proposed) 'tis intended that the Interest of 3 *l.* 10 *s.* *per Cent.* shall be reduced to 3 *l.* *per Cent.* to all those who will pay it in the Land-Bank Bills, which will advance the Credit of the Bank, and consequently their Profit, by enabling them to lend great quantities. A Bank is like a Merchant, whose Gains don't arise from the extravagant Profit of any particular Commodity, but from the greatness of his Trade; for the Retailers get more *per Cent.* than

than the Merchants: *Therefore it will be in the power of the Bank from whence these Bills are issued, to make them more valuable than other Money, by accepting them for more than other Money, and that they will be Gainers thereby.*

Tenth Assertion.

That this Invention falling the Interest of Money, will advance the Rents of Lands.

Proved. That this Invention (succeeding) will fall the Interest of Money, needs no proof: But it hath been made a Question, Whether the falling the Interest of Money will advance the Rents of Lands? And it must be confessed, that Lands already improved to the heighth

heighth, are not capable of this advantage; but most of the Lands in *England* are capable of being improved to double their present Value; in Cities and Towns by Building, and in the Countreys by Planting and Manure, and lye unimproved for want of Money; *Therefore this Invention falling the Interest of Money will advance the Rents of Lands.*

Eleventh Assertion.

That advancing the Value of Lands in the Purchase, is equal to advancing the Rents.

That the falling the Interest of Money advances Lands in the Purchase, needs no Proof: But it hath been a Question, Whether advancing the Lands in purchase be *Proved.*

be an advantage? becauſe the Value of the money for which they are ſold is thereby depreciated: And it is certain that the falling the Intereſt of Money doth depreciate the Value of it, as to the Purchaſe of the Soil of the Lands, but it doth not depreciate it as to the Purchaſe of any Commodities ſevered from the Soil. The Intereſt of Money is an Annual Profit, and therefore doth affect nothing but what hath an Annual Increaſe. The Soil of Land is an Annual Intereſt to the Owner, and therefore the price thereof riſes and falls with the Intereſt of Money, which is Annual: But the Commodities ſevered from the Soil lye all in Principal, and therefore the Intereſt of Money being Annual, doth not affect them. The Price of Corn and Cattle don't riſe and fall with the Intereſt of Money; or or if at any time they happen ſo to do, it is not cauſed by the Rate of Intereſt, but ſome other cauſe which happens at that time; *Therefore the advancing the Value of Lands in the purchaſe is equal to advancing the Rents.* Indeed, if Men were to live with the Beaſts, ranging up and down the Earth, and taking their Food where they found it, Lands would be of no value in reſpect of Sale; but ever ſince the Commencement of the Laws of Property, Money is as neceſſary as Bread; and therefore whether Land will yield a hundred quarters of Corn, or will ſell for as much as will buy it, is equally beneficial to the Owner.

Twelfth Assertion.

That this Invention perfected will extinguish the Interest of Money upon Lands, and thereby make the Lands inestimable.

Proved. The Securities of Lands are now as valuable as money, or else money would not be lent upon them: And the Reason why the Owners are forced to borrow money upon these Securities, is because they can't make money of them: If therefore these Securities could be made Money, there would be no Occasion of borrowing money upon them, and consequently the Interest of money on these Securities would be extinguished, which makes the Lands

Lands to be ineſtimable ; for all Value is by compariſon, two things of equal goodneſs are the value of one another, and the purchaſe of Lands being valued by the rate of the Intereſt of money, if this Intereſt be extinguiſhed, there is nothing left to make the compariſon whereby to value the Lands, and therefore they muſt be ineſtimable. Pleaſure and Profit are all the Accompliſhments of Life; now the natural produce of Lands ſupplyes all the Pleaſures of Life ; and if the Policy of Man can add the profit of money to it, all the accompliſhments of Life are contained in it.

Omne tulit punctum qui miſcuit utile dulci.

But this is the Invention perfected, which we muſt not promiſe our ſelves to ſee. I only men-

mention it, to ſhew that the falling of Intereſt by this Invention, will be a growing improvement to Lands, even to an infinity, whereby to encourage the beginning of the Invention. I know the Mercurial Projectors of the Age skip to the top of their Notions at the firſt jump, like the Mother of *Zebedee*'s Children, who made it her firſt Prayer, that the two higheſt ſeats in Heaven might be reſerved for her two Sons: But this ſhews their ignorance of Nature, *who never leaps*; all aſcent is by climbing, Men grow from Children, Trees from Seeds, and Learning from the Element of Letters; I don't doubt but Lands by this Invention may be advanced to a hundred Years purchaſe; but this muſt proceed from the Practice and Improvement of the Invention, and not the Notion of it only: If the growth

growth of this Invention will yearly advance the value of Land one Years purchaſe, (which may modeſtly be expected) it is in effect doubling the preſent Rents.

Thirteenth Aſſertion.

That though this Improvement added to the preſent Value of Lands be unexpected, and ſurprizing, it is nevertheleſs plain and true, and agreeable to other productions in Nature and Arts: And though it is plain and true, it is never the leſs valuable, but rather the more admirable.

When God had made Man, he **Proved**

gave

gave him a view of all the Creatures made before him, *pleaſant to the eye, and pleaſant to the taſte, and good for food*; which was a compleat Entertainment to him, as he apprehended, for he felt no Appetite in himſelf, but what had a ſuitable Object to gratifie it. And yet all this while Man had within him a dormant Affection, (which he did not know of) capable of a higher Enjoyment than all his other Appetites, and this lay concealed from him, 'till the Creator preſented him with *his Female*; who being an Object ſuited to that Affection, gave him the firſt feeling of it. Love is an Affection contracted by the Eye, and therefore 'till the Object was produced, the Affection lay dormant, (as Fire doth in Stones 'till they are ſmitten): If therefore the *Faireſt Aſpect* of the Creation was preſented to Man, after he had end-

ended his Expectations of being entertained with any more Objects, and consequently *That highest pleasure of Life* was added to him, after he had ended his Expectations of any further happiness, why should it seem strange, that other Qualities in Nature should lye concealed, 'till the Wisdom of Providence thinks fit to produce them. How many things now common in the World were kept hid from Ages past? as the virtue of the Load-stone, and thereby the discovery of *America*, the use of Guns, Printing, Glass, *&c.* The Earth is the great Staple of the World, made by God to be manufactured and improved by Man, and perhaps the things not yet seen are greater than the things already seen. And tho' we can have no Notion of them till they are produced, yet when they are made

to

to appear, the Concealment of them ſeems more miraculous than the Diſcovery, for the making them to appear, makes them plain, and the plain appearance of them raiſes an admiration, that they were never before obſerved. *Inventions are Myſteries found out*, and what is not plain, is not found out, but remains a Myſtery ſtill, ſo that the Author of an Invention (to make it perfect) muſt thereby looſe the Honour of it, and be deſpiſed, as producing a common thing. And that this may be my Fate, is the top of my Ambition; however this proves the Aſſertion, *That tho' this Improvement added to the preſent value of the Lands, ſeem extravagant, and be unexpected and ſurpriſing, it is nevertheleſs plain, and true, and agreable to other Productions in Nature and Arts: And tho' it is plain and true, it is never the leſs valuable, but rather the more admirable.*

Fourteenth

Fourteenth Assertion.

That therefore it can't be doubted but the Legislative Power will encourage this Invention, by reviving the Clauses relating to Lands, in the Act passed last Sessions, for Establishing a Land-Bank.

When we address to our Superiours, for any thing to be done by them, it is Duty and Good Manners to consider, 1st. *That the Notion and Intent of the thing we propose be useful and honest, in case it can be effected.* 2dly. *That the practice of it be made visible and plain, before we offer it:* 3dly. *That we pre-* *Proved.*

pare

pare every thing ready for their Fiat, *which is to give the Sanction*; that they may have nothing to do, but what can be done by none but themselves: Now that the *Notion* and Intent of forming these Securities of Lands into the Qualities of Money, and using them as Money, will be esteemed by the Legislative Power to be useful and honest, in case it can be effected, cannot remain a Doubt. Then the next Query is, *Whether the practice of this Notion can be made visible and plain?* The first part of the Notion is the forming these Securities into the Qualities of Money, and this belongs to him that offers the Invention, for 'tis not the Business of the Legislative Power to draw Settlements and Forms, those must be done by some one of that Science to which these Forms and Settlements relate. And that I may not seem

ſeem to amuſe with implicite terms, this Form is nothing but *Diviſion*: The forming the Securities of Lands into the Qualities of Money, is no more than *Dividing theſe Securities into ſmaller Summs.* Diviſion is the firſt thing in Form. In the Deſcription of the Creation it's ſaid to be without Form, and void, 'till it was divided, *The Light from the Darkneſs, and the Waters from the Dry Land*; and by theſe Lights, Eternity was divided, and ſub-divided into Time, of *Years, Days and Hours*, for Man to keep his Accounts by; for Eternity undivided is of no uſe to Man. Every thing is more or leſs valuable, as 'tis more or leſs capable of Diviſion. Now 'till theſe Securities were made diviſible, all the reſidue of the Invention was impoſſible; for if the Securities themſelves are not capable of being formed ſormed into the Qualities of Money, it is not in the Power of the Parliament to make them ſo. But this firſt Part of the Invention is actually done, and hath ſhewed it ſelf in all the parts of it. The *26th.* of *October*, 1695. was the firſt day of iſſuing out Bills charged upon Lands, (which are the Securities thereof divided) and theſe were the firſt Bills (we hear of) that have been charged upon Lands, and iſſued out for Money: And to give plain Inſtances that theſe Securities, ſo divided into Bills, are Money, the Mortgagees who had theſe Securities before they were divided, and were to receive the Monies due upon them, brought their Securities to the Bank, to be formed into Bills, and received back thoſe Bills for their Money; *They brought the Bullion into the Bank, and took it back in Coin*; and for doing this the

the Owners of the Lands are content to pay a ſmall Intereſt to the Bank, for keeping a Caſh of other Monies, to anſwer theſe Bills as they are demanded, (*and this by the way may ſilence all Enquiries into the profit of the Bank*): And in this manner there has been iſſued out forty five thouſand Pounds in Bills, all which have been paid and repaid as Money, and the Bank had valued Eſtates for iſſuing out One hundred thouſand pounds more, but fore-ſeeing the impoſſibility of maintaining a Credit in their Infancy, during the Regulation of the Coin, they ſtopt their Hands, and content themſelves at preſent in paying their Bills already iſſued, and giving an undeniable demonſtration of the firſt part of the Invention, by forming the Securities of Lands into the Qualities of Money, and thereby ſtanding ready for the Sanction

and

and aſſiſtance of the Legiſlative Power towards the perfecting of this Invention.

What was paſſed by the Act of laſt Seſſions, relating to Lands, and is now humbled repreſented to the Legiſlative Power, is,

Firſt, *That the Subſcribers may be incorporated*, in order to ſtand ſeiz-ed of Lands to be conveyed to them, to prevent the charge or Fraud of Truſtees. In the dividing the Securities of Lands, the Legal Eſtates thereof muſt be conveyed to Truſtees, who are to ſtand ſeiz-ed in the firſt place for the Per-ſons who have the Bills charged on the Lands, and afterwards in truſt for the Owners of the Lands, who make the Conveyances; and to prevent the Legal Eſtates from going to Heirs or Execu-tors, there muſt be ſeveral Truſtees in every Conveyance, which may

occa-

occaſion great Charge and Trouble in transferring the Securities, eſpecially if the Truſtees prove corrupt, (which often happens in common Securities, amongſt private Men) : I have known a Mortgager forced to pay twenty Guineas to a parcel of Truſtees, for ſealing an Aſſignment of his Mortgage : Now this charge of Tranſferring Securities entailed on Freehold Eſtates, is as real Incumbrance upon them as Fines upon alienations are upon Copy-holds : And if (as hath been obſerved) the transferring the Titles of Land to Money, and making the aſſignment of every piece to be by Deed, would depreciate it, and incapacitate it from being Money, by the ſame reaſon the transferring the Titles of Money to Lands, and making the delivery only to be a Title, would (of it ſelf) render them much more

va-

valuable; and tho' the equitable Interests only (which are the Bills) can be assigned by Delivery, yet the less Charge is incident to transferring the Legal Estates, the more valuable the Lands will be, *And this is the Intent of being Incorporated.* A great part of the Towns and Trades in *England* have been incorporated by Kings or Parliaments, for the conveniency of doing their own Business. The *Worsted-Weavers* in *Yarmouth* and *Lynn* were each of them incorporated by Parliament, in 15*th. Hen.* 8. with a power to have a Seal for their own Cloths, for no other reason than that it was before painful and costly for them to carry their Cloths to be sealed at *Norwich*, which they were obliged to by a former Act. And the *School of Norleech in Gloucester-shire* was Incorporated by Parliament, in 4. *Jac.* 1. upon the

Opi-

Opinion of three Lord Keepers, and two Judges, that they ought to be Incorporated, in order to ſtand ſeized of their own Lands; for that the ſurviving Feoffee of the School-Lands went about to defraud the School, by making a long Leaſe to his own Son, under a ſmall Rent. If therefore the Kings and Parliaments of *England* have incorporated ſo many Towns and Trades, for the conveniency of doing their buſineſs, and that the Parliament (in the firſt of theſe Caſes) incorporated two Companies of *Weavers*, for preventing their trouble and charge in going to diſtant places; and (in the laſt Caſe) incorporated a Countrey-School, to prevent frauds in their Truſtees, can it be doubted that the preſent Legiſlative Power will deny the like conveniency for the better ſettling and improving all the Lands in the Kingdom? and

in

in this they have ſignified their pleaſure already, by declaring (in the Act paſſed laſt Seſſions) that the intent of the Incorporation was in order to lending Monies on Lands.

The *Second* Thing contained in the laſt Act, and now humbly repreſented to the Parliament, is, *The ſecuring the Titles of the Lands after they are ſo ſettled*: And this is intended by the Settlement already executed and practiſed, whereby it is declared that the Lands conveyed purſuant to that Settlement, (as long as they ſtand ſo conveyed) ſhall not be ſubject to any other Incumbrances than what ſhall be charged thereon by the Owners thereof, in the Regiſter-Books of the *Bank*; by which the Lawyers are of Opinion, that the Lands will be protected againſt any other future Incumbrance. But to put that

that out of all doubt, it was inserted in the Act, which can be no Unjustice to any, (as a Register with a Retrospect might be) being only the initiating of a voluntary Register, to be perfected by time.

The *Third* Clause relating to Lands in the last Act, and now humbly represented, is, *A power by publick sale to sell the Mortgaged Lands, in case the Money lent thereon by the Bank be demanded, and unpaid six years together*; and with the Money arising by sale to Discharge the Mortgage Monies, returning the Overplus to the Owner of the Lands. And this will save Expences in Suits, which must otherwise be charged on the Lands.

There are other Clauses for Transferring the Bills, Searching of Judgments, *&c.* for the better

Se-

Security and Conveniency of the Bank.

And that this Conſtitution may not be diverted from the end propoſed and intended, we ſhall think it no Penalty that the Bank may be reſtrained from iſſuing out any Bills, but what ſhall be charged upon Lands conveyed unto them, which is more reſtrictive than all the Clauſes drawn for that purpoſe by the late Oppoſers of the Act.

Now all theſe being Conveniencies only, grantable by the Legiſlative Power, without charging any Mans Property, and the uſe of them ſeeming ſo neceſſary and advantagious, *It cannot be doubted but the Legiſlative Power will encourage this Invention, by reviving theſe Clauſes.*

Fifteenth Aſſertion.

That it cannot be doubted but the Owners of the Lands will readily receive and uſe this Invention.

Silver and Gold are Forreign Commodities, bought of thoſe who are ſometimes our Allies, and ſometimes our Enemies, and we (by virtue of our Agreements) have made them Money, to the depreciating the value of our own Lands; and ſhall not we (by the ſame Agreements) make Money of our Lands, which will coſt nothing, and double the value of the Lands by doing it? Never was any thing more eagerly received than Propoſals for lowering the Intereſt of Money, inſomuch that the No- *Proved*

tions

tions of it dispersed in common Pamphlets, brought men out of all Countreys, only to hear silly Men talk about it. Perhaps some Ceremonies may be used in the Order and precedency of coming into this Invention. When that Doctrine (which we now profess to be our Religion) was first vented in the World, the Priests and Rulers stood off, and would not meddle with it, because they were safely posted at the head of the Church and State, and had no occasion to expose their Reputation, by turning Projectors, and venturing upon a new thing, before they knew whether it would take or not; and therefore they set the Publicans and Harlots (who thought themselves to have most need of it) to go in first, to try the Experiment; but when they found that the thing would do, they all fell in to it one after another, 'till at laſt it came to be as ſcandalous to be out of it, as it was at firſt to be in it. I know the thing now propoſed is New, and therefore I expect that thoſe who are a cold muſt firſt blow this Coal, but when 'tis once kindled, it can never want Fuel to maintain the Fire. We call them *Fops* who invent new Faſhions, and yet we all follow them one after another; ſome will have them in a Week, others in a Month, ſome in a Year after they are in, and ſome ſeven Years after they are out; and ſo it is in the change of other Cuſtoms; for if Men ſhould be all of the ſame mind together, the crowd would hinder the doing the buſineſs they come about. Men fall into things one after another, as their Occaſions and Inducements lead them. There is

no

no Profit in the World made certain: All Gain depends upon the contingent Occasions and Necessities of others; a Lawyer is not sure of Clients, nor a Physitian of Patients, nor a Landlord of Tenants, nor a Monied Man of any one to borrow of him, but they all expect the Necessities of others to support themselves by; and *therefore the present Necessities requiring the use of this Invention, it cannot be doubted but the Owners of the Lands will readily receive and use it*; and by so doing they enter into other Mens Labours, their Estates are improved to their Hands, without their Heads or Thoughts. Let but the reservation of their Leases be made thus, *Yielding therefore the Summe of* 100 l. *in Lawful Money of* England, *Or in Bills of the* Land-Bank, and *This short Disjunctive* makes the Bills Lawful Money of

England,

England, and the Owners of the Lands to be Bankers upon the Credit of their own Eſtates.

Sixteenth Aſſertion.

That a General Conſent of the Kingdom to receive and uſe this Invention, would cauſe a ſudden fall of the Price of Money, notwithſtanding the practice and execution of it could not be immediately made general.

By General I don't mean Univerſal, that every Man ſhould ſet his Hand to it, but a common Approbation of it by thoſe who know it. Men deal upon Proſpects of what is like to be: Merchants and *Proved.*

and Ttraders have gotten Eſtates, by foreſeeing the riſe or fall of Commodities, and 'tis obſerved amongſt them, that an extravagant price of any Commodity doth produce a ſudden fall, by putting Mens Heads to work to procure more of the ſame kind, or to invent ſomething elſe inſtead of it. And did the preſent Owners of Money foreſee a fall of it, by providing a Supply of another Species, they would part with it as they do with other Commodities, under the like apprehenſions. There is no way to break Game-Houſes but to keep out of them, nor any way to fall the price of Money, but to leſſen the occaſions of it. *That therefore*, &c.

Seventeenth

Seventeenth Aſſertion.

That the Reviving theſe Clauſes in the beginning of the approaching Seſſions, will almoſt amount to an Unanimous Conſent of the Kingdom to receive and uſe this Invention; and will thereby facilitate the raiſing the preſent Supplyes for the Government, by a ſudden fall of the Price of Money.

It is not intended by reviving theſe Clauſes in the beginning of the Seſſions, that the Supplies of the Government ſhould be poſt-poned, but firſt provided for. The Govern- *Proved.*

ment

ment is the ſence of the Kingdom, without which the Subjects cannot enjoy their Properties, and therefore to provide for our ſelves before the publick, is as if a Man ſhould ſow his Corn before he hath encloſed his Ground. And as our own Security obliges us to provide for future Defence, ſo Juſtice and Gratitude calls for the Arrears of the Army and Navy, who have fought upon the Honour of the Kingdom, to preſerve us at home in Peace; and therefore they who have enjoyed that repoſe, cannot truly call any thing their own, 'till they have made Proviſion to pay the utmoſt Farthing of ſo juſt a Debt.

But the preſent Owners of Monies depending that there will be a Neceſſity of raiſing the value of the Coin, (as the Term is) will not deliver it out of their Poſſeſſion to others, to receive the advan-

tage

tage of the riſe, and 'till this matter be adjuſted, they who want Money muſt pay Extortion inſtead of Intereſt. Now as to the thing it ſelf of raiſing the Coin, to me it ſeems, *As to paſt Contracts*, to be an inverſion of Agreements, (of which I have before wrote my thoughts) and *as to future Contracts*, to be wholly inſignificant, for if I am to repay the ſame Money I receive, 'tis no matter what the weight of it be. And *upon the whole*, it ſeems to have a Trick in it, which muſt be ſhewed but once, like the ſplitting of ſhares in Joint-ſtocks, to multiply them in the Hands of thoſe whoſe they then are, that, before the fallacy is found out, they may ſell them (by number) to others, who come to the right underſtanding of it by the fall of them in their own Hands: By which I would not be thought to reflect on

thoſe

thofe Gentlemen (whofe Opinions have feemed for it) as defigning any ill, for I own that my firft apprehenfions of it were different from what I have now hinted; tho' I never read the Arguments in it, or ever concerned my felf about it; having waived the Study of it, to find out another Species befides it. And therefore I defire that what I have here offered as my prefent Conceptions of it, may not be taken as any part of my Argument.

The Drift of this Effay is to depreciate the Value of our Gold and Silver, as it now is, by making another Species more valuable than that, by the acceptance of it at a higher rate. It is to underfell the *Spaniards*, by making Money of our home Manufacture, without any other charge than fome Paper or Parchment; and if the Legifla-

tive

tive Power (in the beginning of the approaching Sessions) shall be pleased to declare their Resolution against raising the denomination of the value of the Coin, and will second that Resolution with reviving these Clauses, it will almost amount to a general Consent of the Kingdom to receive and use this Invention. An Act of Parliament is an Agreement of the Kingdom; for tho' I have before (by way of Argument) supposed an Act to pass contrary to the Nature of Laws, yet it is not to be supposed that the Wisdom of the Legislative Power will ever do this in Fact. And I dare imitate the Prophet, to fore-tell, That a Bill of Revivor (grounded upon these Reasons) passed into a Law, will cause as sudden and unexpected a fall to the price of Money in *England*, as the Noise heard in the Camp of the

Syri-

Syrians did to the *price of Provisions* in the Seige of *Samaria*, and thereby give occasion to use the Acclamation of the Poet upon another Event,

— *Quod, optanti divum promittere nemo*
Auderet, volvenda dies én attulit ultrò.

What Heaven durst not promise them that pray,
Here's of it self produced in a day.

Eighteenth

Eighteenth Assertion.

That a Settlement of a Bank for Lands distinct by it self, without annexing it to the Supplyes of the Government, seems the best Establishment of it.

The Government wanting their Supplies in Species of Gold and Silver, the Subscriptions for that purpose must be made by those who have the possession of the Money, who being (for the greatest part) Merchants and Traders, must thereby have the first possession of the Bank; and they being unacquainted with the Securities of Lands, and accustomed to more present Gains then low Interest seems to them to be, they will endeavour to divert *Proved* vert their Credit from Lands to what they apprehend more profitable, and of this we have had an Example in the Bank of *England*: Whereas if a Bank for Lands be eſtabliſhed by it ſelf, their Occaſions for Money will ariſe by degrees, and may be raiſed by the Owners of the Land themſelves, either in Money, or in Securities on their Lands, which (by the aſſiſtance of this Invention) will be equally uſeful as Money of Gold or Silver: *That therefore*, &c.

Nineteenth

Nineteenth Aſſertion.

That a Bank thus eſtabliſh-ed, will be a greater Se-curity to the Government for the future, than a Bank ſet up for that pur-poſe only.

Curſed be he that divideth the Intereſt of the Government and People. Private Subjects have all along ſupplied the Government with Money, through the Bank of *England* as their Caſheir, who have taken upon them to diſpoſe of it as their own, and magnified themſelves to the Publick for it, which hath put a Diſobligation upon their Creditors, that thoſe that have only the Receipt of the Money, ſhould **Proved.**

be

be eſteemed the Owners of it: Now in this Bank here propoſed, the Bank lends the Subjects, and enables them to execute the grateful office of lending the Money to the Publick with their own Hands, and to receive the Profit of it, and yet the Bank is as ſerviceable to the Crown, as if they lent them the Money directly, becauſe it is incumbent on the Bank to pay the Bills, which is the moſt difficult part in all Accounts: And is not the Crown more ſecure in being ſupplied by a Bank, whoſe Securities are charged on the Lands, and their Credit, ſupported by the Receipts of the Rents of the Kingdom, than by a Bank to which the King himſelf is forced to give the chiefeſt Credit by receiving their Bills in the publick Revenues, to his loſs? *That therefore a Bank thus eſtabliſhed will be greater Security to the Government for the*

the future, than a Bank ſet up for that purpoſe only.

Twentieth Aſſertion.

That an Unanimous Conſent in this Eſtabliſhment, would be a happy Event of the War.

By the Conſtitution of the Government of *England*, the Execution of the Law is veſted in the Body Politick of the King, that he may ſtand ſeiz'd thereof to the uſe of the Subjects, for preſerving their Liberties and Eſtates; and whenever that Truſt is broken, the Subjects having no Court of Equity to appeal to, are driven to their Arms, and the Deſcent of his preſent Majeſty with his Forreign Troops into *England*, was to head the Subjects againſt *Proved.*

gainst the Invasion of their Liberties, begun upon them by him, who then had the possession of the Crown, which being translated to his present Majesty, put him into the possession of the Law, and thereby the Subjects into the use of their Liberties under him. But to maintain this Possession, it was absolutely necessary to begin the War against a Forreign Power, who had made themselves formidable by unjust acquisitions from their Neighbours; and this War hath and will cost us forty Millions of Money, directly advanced to maintain it, besides the Losses by Sea, and yet 'tis the best Money that ever the Subjects spent; for by this they have preserved the whole, which otherwise had been lost before now, and therefore according to that Saying, *What is saved is got*, the Expence and Loss of the War hath purchased three

three Kingdoms, with which we may rest well satisfied, without the fond Conceipt of the Conquest of *France*, which is to ask we know not what.

But as a Reward to the Subjects for their Zeal and Bravery in expending so large a part of their present Possessions, to convey the Reversion of their Estates and Liberties to their Posterity, here seems a fair Opportunity offer'd (occasion'd by the Expence of the War) for improving their own Estates, with their Wives and Families at home, which is better than transplanting themselves to Forreign Conquests. Would but the Gentlemen of *England* for one Year spend as much time and pains in their several Countyes to promote this Invention, as they do to manure two Acres of Land, they would find the Improvements increasing

creaſing upon them a ſufficient Encouragement to proceed in it, 'till they had made themſelves rich, and from their abundance the Neceſſities of the Poor would be ſupplyed. I can ſay truly, that the Miſeries of the Poor do affect me, and yet I never had thoughts of Propoſing any thing directly for their Releif, apprehending their chiefeſt dependance to be upon the Superfluities of the rich ; and this was the Proviſion made for them by the firſt Law of the World, which forbid the rakeing of the Corn, that the Poor might live upon the Gleanings, and the leavings of the Poor is the Proviſion for the Fowls of the Air — Whereas raiſing the Rates for the Poor, without adding ſomething to thoſe that are taxed, doth inſenſibly draw the Scot and Lot-men into the Poors-book, the Rates mulitiplying

ing the Poor as faſt as the Poor multiply the Rates — But let more be given to them who have the poſſeſſion of much already, and ſomewhat of it will naturally fall to them that have nothing.

As for the *King* himſelf, (whoſe Succeſs is our Safety) I can't conceive him capable of any greater or leſs Enjoyment than his own Complacency in that Choice which hath deſcended upon him from Providence, to be the *Deliverer* of that People who have alſo choſen him for their *Defender*: And tho' his *Allyance by Blood* be the initiating of his Title to the Crown, yet his *Election* thereunto is his higheſt Perſonal Honour. *To be a King* is a mean thing in compariſon of being *made* one. The *Redeemer of the World* was an Office of that ſtate and dignity, that his *Harbinger* is declared to be the high-

highest post of Honour that ever Man stood possessed of, and yet 'tis said of this Redeemer, *He gloryed not that he was an High Priest, but that he was* made *an High Priest*: He did not magnifie himself that he *was* the Redeemer of the World, but that he was *Chosen by God* to be so.

And I am glad to find my Arguments terminate here, for by this I know I have done, because I have run it where I can go no further: Nor did I know what I was going to do, when I first put Pen to Paper, or where I should begin or end, but having seen and (for some years) felt the extravagant rate of Money, I resolved to search the Pedigree of it, (as Men do of Upstarts preferred above their Merit) and if I should find it of an Honourable Descent

Deſcent, and abſolutely neceſſary, I reſolved to conceal it, but if I could trace its Original to be mean and inconſiderable, I reſolved to expoſe it, thereby to vilifye it in Mens Thoughts, as not ſo indiſpenſably neceſſary as 'tis generally apprehended: Not but that Money is abſolutely neceſſary, but not the very Money of Gold and Silver. And in purſuit of this Enquiry, I found that tho' the common uſe of this (as of other things) be obvious unto all, yet when we would diſſect them, to ſearch out the manner of their Subſiſtence and Operations, we find them all faſtned down to the Root of Nature, by certain Fibers, which we muſt digg down to, and trace from thence into all the Labyrinths of Succeſſion, feeling all our way by that thread. There are no Fractions in Nature, nor any things independant, they are all linked

linked to one another in a continued Chain, which reaches from the Creation to Eternity: And I have ſo far endeavoured to imitate Nature in what I have written, as to argue from a Chain of Poſitions, ſucceſſively depending upon one another, which is the moſt dangerous way of arguing, becauſe if one Poſition happens to be falſe, it vitiates all that follow: But there is no finding out the Truth any other way. 'Tis an eaſie matter to frame Sentences, and dance up and down with them and never be diſcovered whether they are true or falſe, becauſe the Notions are not digeſted into ſuch a Method, that either the Writer or Reader can judge of them: But when the Aſſertions are poſitive, and the Arguments to prove them follow immediately upon them, the Writer and Reader can the better judge of them, as they go along; and if every individual be true by it self, then the whole is true altogether, or else not. And upon review of what I have written, it all seems to me to be true, or else I would not publish it; but yet my Arguments may be fantastical and fallacious, tho' I don't know it, therefore I offer them to be scanned by others.

Truth made manifest is the Foundation I have aimed at, and tho' my Assertions seem bold, I hope my Proofs do manifest them to be true; and it in finding out the Truth I have spoken more plainly and freely of some things that have fallen into my Arguments, than otherwise I should do, I hope the Truth found out will excuse my manner of Enquiry after it.

And to clench the Nail, I'll venture to fling in a bolder Assertion than all the rest, *That there is no other*

Foun-

Foundation to build and support the Credit of the Kingdom upon, than the very thing hereby proposed: But this being a Negative, I'll let it stand to be falsifyed by those who will prove the contrary, by doing it. Nor do I say that there is nothing else to be done, but that this ought not to be left undone, for tho' the present Supplies could be otherwise raised, the growing Interest of Money will eat out the Kingdom, unless something be laid to the Root of it, to eat out that. The Interest of Money hath such a *Spell* in it, that were the whole Coin of the Kingdom but ten thousand Pounds, the Rate of Interest for that Summ would set a price upon all the Lands in *England*, which are computed at 15 Millions *per Annum*; and the less principal Money there is, the higher the Interest rises, therefore there is no way to

fall

fall the Intereſt but to multiply the Principal. *In the time of the Late Revolutions*, upon reading a Bill in the Houſe of *Commons*, Entituled, *An Ordinance for ſuppreſſing the Horrible Sin of Adultery*, a Member there moved that the Title might be, *An Ordinance for the more ſecret committing the Horrible Sin of Adultery* : And conſidering how Uſury and Extortion have thriven under all the Laws made againſt them, the Titles of the Acts for that purpoſe might have been, *For the more Artificial taking Extortion and Uſury.* Now in multiplying the Principal of Money, perhaps other Securities may be ſo formed, as to ſupply the uſe of Monies as well as the Securities on Lands. But the Credit of them muſt depend upon their Alliance with Lands, eſpecially ſince the Owners of the Lands (having Intimation of their Strength) will

be

be able to suppress any Credit that shall be set up in Prejudice to their Estates.

And after all this, had I not a greater Authority to justifie my Assertions than all the Arguments I have used to prove them, I durst not be so bold; but that I may not seem immodest by taking so much upon me, I own my self ignorant of many other Accomplishments, that I might attain to this, I have waved all Advantages in my Profession, to study *A more convenient Settlement for Lands*; and therefore I hope the more Learned and Successful in that Science will not envy me, if I should be the Author of an Improvement in that point, and thereby entail upon my self the Despicable Name of a Projector for doing it: However *as to that*, every Man is either a *Projector*, by finding out New Forms, or a *Mechanick*,

chanick by copying after them: And if they who give me the Character of the former, will please to accept the Title of the latter, I shall not think my self affronted: Especially since the *Sages of the Law* themselves, who have chosen that grave Sentence for their Motto, *Nolumus Leges Angliæ mutare*, have been the Projectors of New Inventions in the Law, which by time have grown into Customs. The Titles of the greatest part of the Lands in *England* do depend upon an Invention of the Lawyers, in the manner of passing Recoveries to bar Estates Tail, notwithstanding the Statute of *Westminster* 2nd. For tho' the Writs on which these Recoveries are grounded, were ancient, yet the setting up a *Common Vouchee*, the Appearance of all Parties *without Proces*, Execution and Seisin and Returns of the Writs *being*

ing

ing all done together in an instant, is a Project in the Law which by Custom hath gained the Name of *A Common Recovery*, and is now become a Common Assurance of Lands. And as the Titles of Lands do thus depend upon an Invention in the Law, so the manner now used for trying these Titles by Possessory Actions, (*termed Ejectments*) is an Invention in the Law, by the introducing of which the antient way of Tryals by *real Actions* is become so obsolete, That *at a Call of Serjeants* the Counts and Pleadings in *Formedons* being transcribed from Precedents, are delivered to these Graduates, only to be read over by them, *as Reliques of the Law*, amongst other *Antiquated Ceremonies* used at that Solemnity.

And if any thing be expected from me, relating to the differences which have happened from

passing

paſſing the Act laſt Seſsions, I muſt ſay no more of it here, than *That* all the Charges and Aſperſions caſt upon us from thence, and the impeaching the Juſtice of the Parliament for eſtabliſhing another Bank, while THE Bank of *England* (whoſe Name or Eſſence never extended beyond 1200000 *l.* limitted them by the Act) is in being, are ſo vain and ridiculous, that *to bind them up with the Names of God and the King*, (whom I have dared to inſert in this Eſſay) would render me guilty of prophaneneſs and irreverence.

Lincolns-Inn,
Septemb. 1696.

J. Aſgill.